PRESENTED TO EMILY STRINGER
ON THE OCCASION OF YOUR
BAPTISM ON JANUARY 8TH,
1995 AT ST STEPHEN'S
ANGLICAN CHURCH IN
WEST VANCOUVER, B.C BY
REV. KEITH GILBERT

   WITH LOVE
   GRANPA.
      Gordon Stringer

The Prayer Garden

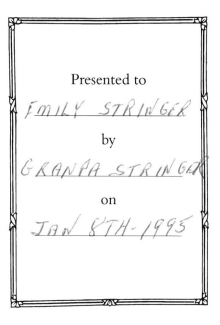

Presented to

EMILY STRINGER

by

GRANPA STRINGER

on

JAN 8TH - 1995

The Prayer Garden

An anthology of Children's Prayers

CHRISTOPHER HERBERT

HarperCollins*Publishers*

HarperCollins*Religious*
Part of HarperCollins*Publishers*
77—85 Fulham Palace Road, London W6 8JB

First published in Great Britain
in 1994 by HarperCollins*Religious*

1 3 5 7 9 10 8 6 4 2

A catalogue record for this book is
available from the British Library

ISBN 0 551 02812-2

Phototypeset by Harper Phototypesetters Limited,
Northampton, England
Printed and bound in Great Britain by
HarperCollinsManufacturing Glasgow

Contents

Introduction

You know what it's like when people don't listen to you. They may seem to be listening, but you know they're not really. It leaves you feeling miserable and perhaps a bit angry.

But think of those people who truly listen to you, the ones who give you their full attention. It's a marvellous feeling. You feel loved and respected.

Praying to God is like talking to someone who really understands, someone who has all the time there is to listen to the things that matter to you. You can tell God about what makes you happy or sad. You can tell God about what frightens you or what makes you laugh.

You can tell God anything, anything at all, and be certain that he will listen to you carefully. God listens to you because he loves you.

He may not answer your prayers in the way you think he should, but he will listen and will show you what you ought to do. Sometimes he uses stories from the Bible to show us his answers, sometimes his answer comes through other people, sometimes he makes us certain in our own minds about what we must do.

The best way of praying is to use your own words. You can talk to God as naturally as if you were talking to your best friend. Sometimes the words and prayers other people have used can be helpful too.

Here in this book is a collection of prayers to help you pray, to help you draw close to God, to help you know his love.

Prayer is a way of talking to God, knowing that he loves you very much and listens to all you say.

The Lord's Prayer

The Lord's Prayer

Jesus spent a lot of time praying. He sometimes went off to a quiet place on his own and there he spoke with God.

His friends asked him to teach them to pray. And Jesus replied by giving them his own special prayer. We call it 'The Lord's Prayer'. There are many versions of this prayer. The traditional one is this:

Our Father, who art in heaven,
Hallowed be thy name.
Thy kingdom come,
Thy will be done,
On earth as it is in heaven.
Give us this day our daily bread,
And forgive us our trespasses
As we forgive those who trespass
   against us.
Lead us not into temptation,
But deliver us from evil.
For thine is the kingdom,
The power and the glory,
For ever and ever,
Amen.

BOOK OF COMMON PRAYER

A more modern version is this:

Our Father in heaven,
Hallowed be your name.
Your kingdom come,
Your will be done,
On earth as in heaven.
Give us today our daily bread,
And forgive us our sins,
As we forgive those who sin against us.
Lead us not into temptation,
But deliver us from evil,
For the kingdom, the power and the
    glory are yours,
Now and for ever,
Amen.

ALTERNATIVE SERVICE BOOK

It is good to say the Lord's Prayer every day, and to learn it off by heart.

Prayer is a way of talking to God, knowing that he is like a loving parent.

Beginnings

Beginnings

Every day is a new beginning. No one has ever lived the day before. It's clean, shining, waiting to be explored, full of surprises – both exciting and scary.

So it's important to begin each day by trusting ourselves to the care of God. There is no place we can go where God will not be with us. Nothing can happen to us without God being willing to share it.

We begin each day with God. We go through each day with God. And we end each day with God.

Prayer is a way of walking each day with God.

In the beginning, when God created the universe, the earth was formless and desolate. The raging ocean that covered everything was engulfed in total darkness, and the power of God was moving over the water.

GENESIS 1:1–2

In the sixth month of Elizabeth's pregnancy God sent the angel Gabriel to a town in Galilee named Nazareth. He had a message for a girl promised in marriage to a man named Joseph, who was a descendant of King David. The girl's name was Mary. The angel came to her and said, 'Peace be with you! The Lord is with you and has greatly blessed you!'

Mary was deeply troubled by the angel's message, and she wondered what his words meant. The angel said to her, 'Don't be afraid, Mary; God has been gracious to you. You will become pregnant and give birth to a son, and you will name him Jesus. He will be great and will be called the Son of the Most High God. The Lord God will make him a king, as his ancestor David was, and he will be the king of the descendants of Jacob for ever; his kingdom will never end!'

LUKE 1:26–33

The eleven disciples went to the hill in Galilee where Jesus had told them to go. When they saw him, they worshipped him, even though some of them doubted. Jesus drew near and said to them, 'I have been given all authority in heaven and on earth. Go, then, to all peoples everywhere and make them my disciples: baptise them

8

in the name of the Father, the Son and the Holy Spirit, and teach them to obey everything I have commanded you. And I will be with you always, to the end of the age.'

MATTHEW 28:16–20

∿

When the day of Pentecost came, all the believers were gathered together in one place. Suddenly there was a noise from the sky which sounded like a strong wind blowing, and it filled the whole house where they were sitting. Then they saw what looked like tongues of fire which spread out and touched each person there. They were all filled with the Holy Spirit and began to talk in other languages, as the Spirit enabled them to speak.

ACTS 2:1–4

∿

Another day
Give us this day our daily discovery.

DR RENDELL HARRIS: *ANOTHER DAY,* CARDEN

∿

Beauty
O Christ, we come into thy presence, and how beautiful it is! There is no place so beautiful as the place where thou art.

A PRAYER FROM INDIA: *ANOTHER DAY,* CARDEN

∿

Together

Lord, help me to remember that
nothing is going to happen today that
you and I cannot handle together.

ANOTHER DAY, CARDEN

~

Let your spirit be my sail

O Jesus,
Be the canoe that holds me to the sea
 of life.
Be the steer that keeps me on the
 straight road.
Be the outrigger that supports me in
 times of great temptation.
Let your spirit be my sail that carries
 me through every day.
Keep my body strong,
so that I can paddle steadfastly on,
in the long voyage of life.

PRAYERS FOR PILGRIMS, PAWLEY

~

Wherever I go, there God is

There is no place
Where God is not;
Wherever I go, there God is.
Now and always He upholds
Me with his power,
And keeps me safe in
His Love.

BRYN A. REES: PRAYERS FOR PILGRIMS, PAWLEY

~

The path ahead
Bless to me, O God, the earth beneath
  my feet,
Bless to me, O God, the path whereon
  I go,
Bless to me, O God, the people whom
  I meet,
Today, tonight and tomorrow. Amen.

IONA COMMUNITY: *PRAYERS FOR PILGRIMS*, PAWLEY

~

A new day
O God,
I open my eyes to another brand-new,
clean and shiny day;
and I know that whatever happens
you will be with me
giving me strength,
bringing me laughter,
and helping me to live my life to the
  full.

~

Creation

Creation

Think of a time when you were very happy – so happy you could have turned a cartwheel, so happy that you wanted to hug the whole world.

Don't you think that God must have been very happy when he made the world? Imagine the joy of inventing rainbows. Imagine the laughter in heaven when waterfalls, puppies, elephants, snowflakes and robins came into the mind of God.

There is so much happiness in creation, so much beauty. (There is sadness too – and we'll come to that in a later section.) But for the moment look out at the world, look up at the stars, and look deep into the way things are made. And as you look, become aware that God made all of this with love.

Prayer is a way of sharing with God the enjoyment of creation.

~

This is the story of the creation of the sky and the earth. When the Lord God made the earth and the sky, there were no plants on the earth. Nothing was growing in the fields. The Lord God had not yet made it rain on the land. And there was no man to care for the the ground. But a mist often rose from the earth and watered all the ground.

Then the Lord God took dust from the ground and formed man from it. The Lord breathed the breath of life into the man's nose. And the man became a living person. Then the Lord God planted a garden in the East, in a place called Eden. He put the man he had formed in that garden. The Lord God caused every beautiful tree and every tree that was good for food to grow out of the ground. In the middle of the garden, God put the tree that gives life. And he put there the tree that gives the knowledge of good and evil.

GENESIS 2:4–9
INTERNATIONAL CHILDREN'S BIBLE

∾

Praise the Lord from heaven,
you that live in the heights above.
Praise him, all his angels,
all his heavenly armies.

Praise him, sun and moon;
praise him, shining stars.
Praise him, highest heavens,
and the waters above the sky.

Let them all praise the name of the
  Lord!
He commanded, and they were created;
by his command they were fixed in
  their places for ever,
and they cannot disobey.

Praise the Lord from the earth,
sea-monsters and all ocean depths;
lightning and hail, snow and clouds,
strong winds that obey his command.

Praise him, hills and mountains,
fruit trees and forests;
all animals, tame and wild,
reptiles and birds.

Praise him, kings and all peoples,
princes and all other rulers;
girls and young men,
old people and children too.

Let them all praise the name of the
  Lord!
His name is greater than all others;
his glory is above earth and heaven.
He made his nation strong,
so that all his people praise him —
the people of Israel, so dear to him.

Praise the Lord!

PSALM 148, GOOD NEWS BIBLE

17

Harmony with nature
God of the green pastures and still
  waters,
help my heart to beat in time with
the quiet music of your creation.

~

Thanks for creation
Almighty God, King of the Universe,
open our eyes to the glory of your
  creation,
to the planets and the stars,
the seas and the sky,
and give us thankful hearts,
through Jesus Christ our Lord.

~

God in everything
God, you are our father and our
  mother,
you give life to all that exists;
thank you for the gift of our wonderful
  world;
for the gift of ourselves —
and for all whom we love.

The stillness of the mountains
Strong they are, and very quiet
the mountains that reach up to the sky.
I watch the shadows of the clouds
race silently across their slopes,
and give thanks to you, O God,
for the playful power
of your creation.

~

Let there be light
Let there be light:
The light of the moon
The light of the stars
The light of the sun
Light on the waters
Light in the clouds
Light in the mountains
Light on the leaves of the shimmering
    trees.
Let there be light . . . and it was good.
We rejoice, O God, in the light.

~

Creator of Light
O God, Creator of Light: at the rising
    of your sun
this morning, let the greatest of all
    light,
your love,
rise like the sun within our hearts.

MORNING, NOON & NIGHT

~

God as creator
He prayeth best who loveth best
All things both great and small,
For the dear God who loveth us,
He made and loveth all.

S. T. COLERIDGE

～

Sleep in peace
O Heavenly Father, protect and bless all
things that have breath: guard them
from all evil and let them sleep in
peace.

ALBERT SCHWEITZER

～

Beauty
O God, you are great and wonderful,
and show yourself to us in the huge
beauty of the universe and the tiny
beauty of atoms: open my eyes to see
you in all things, and when I see you,
to praise your holy name with all my
heart.

ADAPTED FROM A PRAYER OF ISIDORE OF SEVILLE

～

Litany of thanks
For flowers that bloom about our feet,
Father, we thank thee,
For tender grass so fresh, so sweet,
Father, we thank thee,
For song of bird and hum of bee,

～

For all things fair we hear or see,
Father in heaven, we thank thee.

For blue of stream and blue of sky,
Father, we thank thee,
For pleasant shade of branches high,
Father, we thank thee,
For fragrant air and cooling breeze,
For the beauty of the blooming trees,
Father in heaven, we thank thee.

For this new morning with its light,
Father, we thank thee,
For rest and shelter of the night,
Father, we thank thee,
For health and food, for love and
    friends,
For everything thy goodness sends,
Father in heaven, we thank thee.

RALPH WALDO EMERSON

～

The Cherry Tree
Sitting up here on the cherry tree,
A lot of God's wonderful world I see,
A lot of God's interesting people too,
Busily doing what people do.
Over the fence clean laundry is blowing,
Next door a man is digging and
    hoeing.
They're sizzling something across the
    way,
A barbecue must be planned for today.

21

～

Further away in a field of clover,
Playful puppies roll over and over.
When I climb higher I really can see
The church in a square, and the
    chestnut tree.
There are trucks, cars and buses rushing
    about,
While people pop into the shops or pop
    out.
Dear God, I am thinking it's fun to be
    me
Seeing your world from the top of a tree.

HELLO GOD, WINN

~

Beautiful world
Father, you have made the world very
    beautiful.
Teach us to love our world
and to treat it with reverence and with
    care,
for Jesus' sake.

~

Caring for animals
Give to us all, O Lord, a compassionate
and understanding heart that we may
care for all the creatures of the earth;
not hurting them by cruelty, nor
neglecting them, not abusing them, but
sharing with them in the diverse
wonder of your world.

AUTHOR UNKNOWN

~

On top of a mountain
Lord, I climbed up a huge mountain
and from the top I could look down on
  the birds,
look down on the trees
and look down on the villages far away.
I had never been up so high before.
Thank you for letting me see your
  world in a new and lovely way.

~

Looking at colours
Thank you, Lord, for all the rainbows
  of the world —
the rainbows in flowers
the rainbows in streets
the rainbows in traffic
the rainbows in faces.
We praise and bless you for a rainbow-
  ful world.

~

Sea and sand
Dear God,
the wind from the sea is blowing in my
  hair,
the sand is warm beneath my feet,
and the waves are falling gently on the
  beach;
on such a day,
in such a place,
what can I do except say 'thank you',
Creator and lover of the world.

23

~

Sheer fun
I have a special den,
it's dark and small
and no one is allowed in
except for my best friends
and then we talk and make up passwords.
And when we are bored of that
we go outside and play games
or roar around on our bikes,
but somehow the time for play is never
    long enough.
O God,
I bless and thank you for the sheer fun
of being able to play.

༄

Snowballing
The snow whizzes through the air. Our
hands get so cold we could cry and the
world is a mixture of crazy happiness
and freezing pain. Dear God, bless
those who find snow a real danger and
keep them safe.

༄

White and pink and blue
When we have good weather we wear
    these colours . . .
For the lightness of our summer clothes
For being able to move so much more
    easily
For the joy of summer freedom
We thank you, dearest God.

24

༄

Sea

Far out at sea the white horses toss,
near at hand onto the rocks
the waves crash and hiss and roar:
the sea is a great and wonderful
 mystery to me,
O Lord.
It reminds me of your power
and very great beauty.

~

Energy for life

The water comes crashing down the
mountain turning waterwheels, driving
turbines, giving us energy for our work
and our play. Come to us, Lord, like
that, and fill our lives with the energy
of your Holy Spirit, that we may bring
your life to others.

~

Climbing a rock

Lord, I saw a man climbing up a steep
rock and I felt frightened. When things
happen to me that are a bit scary like
climbing rocks, help me to remember
that you are always with me, protecting
and guiding me with your love.

~

Blessing of the sea

Lord,
I sing your praise,
The whole day through until the night.

25

~

Dad's nets are filled,
I have helped him.
We have drawn them in,
Stamping the rhythm with our feet,
The muscles tense.
We have sung your praise.
On the beach, there were our mammies,
Who brought the blessing out of the
   nets,
Out of the nets into their baskets.
They rushed to the market,
Returned and brought again.
Lord, what a blessing is the sea
With fish in plenty.
Lord, that is the story of your grace.
Lord, with your praise we drop off to
   sleep.
Carry us through the night,
Make us fresh for the morning.
Hallelujah for the day!
And blessing for the night!

OXFORD BOOK OF PRAYER

I am so fortunate

I am so fortunate

Homeless children
I have seen their pictures on the
    television,
children with nowhere to go,
sleeping in cardboard boxes on the
    pavements.
O God, why is this world so mixed
    up?
Some of us have too much; some of us
have too little.
Show me what I can do
to make the world a fairer place.

I don't like
I don't like toads, spiders, rats or snakes.
Sorry, Lord, but there it is . . .
There are times when I don't
    understand your creation.
The ugly things.
The weird things.
They puzzle me.
Why did you create them?
Fun?

Despair?
Mistake?
I'm baffled . . .

~

God's gift
Dear Lord,
you have given us such a rare and
  beautiful world,
help us to treat your creation
as a gift,
and to reverence life
with thankfulness
in all we think and speak and do.

~

Fireworks
The Catherine wheel spins in a whirl of
  light,
the Roman candle juggles with bursting
  colours,
the Vesuvius roars and crackles and
  spurts,
the rockets whoosh up into the dark
  night sky,
and sparklers fizz with excitement.
For the joy and glory of fireworks
I praise you, mighty Lord.

~

Sport
Tennis racket, baseball bat,
rugby football, riding hat,
swimming costume, cricket stumps,

30

~

cycling helmet, skateboard jumps.
O Lord, for these and all our fun
We thank you each and every one.

~

In the park
In the park
a dog barks,
some boys are chasing a football,
some girls are running to the
    swimming pool,
old people sit on benches in the sun
and it's a good place to be.
Bless you, O God, for the makers of
    parks.

~

Football
I lie in the bath
soaking the mud off my knees
and remembering the goal I almost
    scored,
and the time I passed the ball
brilliantly (though no one saw),
and the way I made space for myself —
and I'm just glad, O God,
glad to be alive. Thank you.

~

Tennis
I've tried grunting when I serve
to see if it helps;
I even wear wrist-bands
and a head band

31

~

but I still can't volley like I want to . . .
O God,
bless you for all the things I can do
but please give me the patience
to improve . . .
soon.

∾

Ski-ing
Thank you, God, for the snow on the
  mountains —
for skis and toboggans,
for bright warm clothes
and the wind blowing on my face.
Thank you for all the gifts you have
  given us
and help us to enjoy them to the full,
our Creator and most loving Lord.

∾

Blessing of food
Lord God, the bread of life,
You give us food to eat,
Be with us in our work and play,
And guard us while we sleep.

PUFFIN BOOK OF PRAYER

∾

The loveliness of things
O God of earth and sky and sea
Open our eyes that we may be
Aware of love at the heart of life
Christ's power and strength redeeming
  strife.

∾

And as we eat and drink this day
May all we think and do and say
Be blessed and hallowed without limit
By Father, Son and Holy Spirit.

~

God is great
For food and friendship,
warmth and love,
we bless you, heavenly Father.

~

Whenever I sit down to eat
Whenever I sit down to eat,
Dear Lord, I must think of the needy,
and not gobble up like a gannet,
A bird who is remarkably greedy.

HELLO GOD, WINN

~

For food to eat
For food to eat, and those who prepare
    it
For health to enjoy it, and friends to
    share it,
We thank you, O Lord.

HELLO GOD, WINN

~

I love eating
Lord Jesus,
I love eating apples and
peaches and ripe plums.
Please help me grow like you,
so my life bears the good

33

~

rich fruit of love and kindness,
peace and joy.

HELLO JESUS, SAYER

~

For animals suffering
Hear our humble prayer, O God, for
  our friends the animals,
especially for animals who are
  suffering;
For all that are overworked and
  underfed and cruelly treated;
for all wistful creatures in captivity that
  beat against their bars;
for any that are hunted or lost or
  deserted or frightened or hungry;
for all that are in pain or dying;
for all that must be put to death.
We ask for them all thy mercy and pity,
and for those who deal with them we
  ask a heart of compassion and gentle
  hands and kindly words.
Make us ourselves to be true friends to
  animals,
and so to share the blessing of the
  merciful,
for the sake of thy Son the
  tenderhearted,
Jesus Christ, our Lord.

AUTHOR UNKNOWN

Protection of the environment
This world, O Lord, is so beautiful.
Like a jewel it floats through space
radiant with glory.
Help us to so live in the world
that we may not harm it,
but work with the powers of creation
to bring healing and justice and peace.

~

Birds
Lord, Creator of the eagle and the
sparrow, the dove and the humming
bird, we praise and thank you for the
varied beauty of the birds, their songs
and their flight.

Help us to care for this marvellous
part of your creation; for your name's
sake.

WORDS FOR WORSHIP, MICHAEL DAVIS

~

Pets
Father, thank you for our pets.
We love our dogs, our cats, our
    gerbils . . .
Thank you that they give us so much
    fun.
May we look after them wisely for you
    have entrusted them to us.

~

Fish

Lord, just as our fish rest gently in the
water,
may we rest gently on your unending
love.

~

Blessing on animals

Dear Father, hear and bless
The beasts and singing birds,
And guard with tenderness
Small things that have no words.

ANON

~

A safari park

For the gentleness of giraffes
We thank you Lord
For the mischief of monkeys
We thank you Lord
For the babble of baboons
We thank you Lord
For the equanimity of elephants
We thank you Lord.

~

Dolphins

Thank you, Lord, for dolphins
that dance and dart through the water.
Help us to understand and care for
them
so that our world remains a treasure-
house of beauty.

~

The tortoise
Lord, may we wear the armour of faith
and like the tortoise take pains about all
　we do,
learning that if we live slowly
we may the more appreciate your
　world.

≈

Cats
Our cats are called . . .
We love it when they purr; when they
　scratch;
when they bask in the sun.
Thank you, God, for the grace and the
　beauty and
the mystery of cats.

≈

Dogs
Our dogs are called . . .
We love it when they play; when they
　romp;
when they wag their tails.
Thank you for the huggy friendship of
　our dogs.

≈

A brilliant day
Today, O Lord, is a brilliant day,
a jewel of a day,
a joy of a day,
because I'm getting a new pet.
May I care for my pet with real love

≈

so that together
we may rejoice in the surprises and
  wonders
of your glorious world.

∼

For all animals
Animals in zoos, in films, in books;
hundreds, thousands with different
  looks:
the monkey and the kangaroo,
the eagle and the cockatoo;
the tall giraffe, the crawling snail,
the tiny mouse, the giant whale;
the bear, the emu and the gnat,
the crab, the donkey and the bat.
Thank you for them, large and small,
thank you, God, who made them all.

LET'S PRAY TOGETHER, G. MARSHALL-TAYLOR

∼

Prayer for a sick animal
Father in heaven,
You know that my pet is sick.
I don't know what to do,
and I am very worried.
I know that my prayers
may not make much difference
but I know that you care for
every living thing,
and somehow will comfort us all.

∼

The death of a pet
Lord God, Father and creator of us all,
  thank you for . . .
We feel very sad. Through our own
sadness help us to understand the
sadness of others and try to make the
world a kinder place.

~

A miscellany of animals
O God, I thank thee
for all the creatures thou hast made,
so perfect in their kind —
great animals like the elephant and the
  rhinoceros,
humorous animals like the camel and
  the monkey,
friendly ones like the dog and the cat,
working ones like the horse and the ox,
timid ones like the squirrel and the
  rabbit,
majestic ones like the lion and the tiger,
for birds with their songs.
O Lord, give us such love for thy
  creation
that love may cast out fear,
and all thy creatures see in man
their priest and friend
through Jesus Christ our Lord.
OXFORD BOOK OF PRAYER, GEORGE APPLETON

~

Making music

O Lord, there are times when making
  music is a real struggle:
I can't read the notes, I can't keep time,
and my fingers won't do what I want
  them to.
And there are other times (not so often)
  when everything goes well
and I enjoy it more than I can say.
Give me patience and perseverance
  when things are tough and a thankful
  heart when it all comes together.

∼

Hearing

Blessed Lord, we thank you for the gift
of hearing. Grant that our ears may be
open to all loveliness: to music, and the
laughter of our friends; to running
water; to the wind in the trees; to the
call of the birds and beasts — and to all
the multitude of voices in your strange
creation.

Grant that we may ever hear in them
the music of your love and goodness
and power; through Jesus Christ our
Lord.

PRAYERS FOR EVERYDAY, VICARS BELL

My neighbour

I am glad you made my neighbour
different from me; a different coloured
skin, a different shaped face; a different
response to you. I need my neighbour
to teach me about you; he knows all
the things I don't know.

MONICA FURLONG

~

God bless Africa

God bless Africa,
Guard her children,
Guide her rulers,
And give her peace,
For Jesus Christ's sake.

ARCHBISHOP TREVOR HUDDLESTON

~

Our world

Every one of us is a part of the
    continent,
a part of the mainland;
Not one of us, an island.

We are men and women, one world
    household,
Participating in the life of the
    mainland —

~

In our family,
  our neighbourhood
  our community
  our nation
  our community of nations.

We are none of us an island.

M. A. THOMAS: *ANOTHER DAY*, CARDEN

∼

Contrasts in the world
What a world, O God, you have given
  to us —
from the ice and snow at the north
  pole
to the steaming jungles of the tropics;
from the glaring heat of the deserts
to the lush meadows of temperate
  lands;
from the crags and rocks of huge
  mountains
to the deepest valleys hidden in the
  ocean.
Thank you for the differences.
Thank you for the variety.
Thank you for the wonder.
Keep our minds and hearts open to
  your glory
hidden everywhere.

∼

The hungry

Our prayer, Lord, is that we shall do
something to feed the hungry and
shall work for justice in the world,
through Jesus Christ our Lord.

~

Miserable and hungry

I get so miserable when I'm hungry,
and I look for chocolate
or a canned drink;
Give me the patience to realize
that many people are hungry all the
    time
and cannot get enough to eat.
Let us learn, O God, to share our food
one with another and make this world
    a happier place.

~

Thank you

Thank you, Lord,
for the food we eat,
for the clothes we wear,
for the games we play.
Help us never to forget
those who have little food to eat,
and few clothes to wear,
and no strength for playing games.

~

Help us to serve
Make us worthy, Lord, to serve our
fellow human beings throughout the
world who live and die in poverty and
hunger. Through our hands, grant them
this day their daily bread; and by our
understanding love, give them peace
and joy. Amen.

CO-WORKERS OF MOTHER TERESA: *ANOTHER DAY,*

CARDEN

44

The Seasons

The Seasons

In praise of autumn
We praise you, God, for golden leaves.
We praise you, God, for gentle mists.
We praise you, God, for apples and
  fruit.
We praise you, God, for chestnuts and
  conkers.
We praise you, God, for a glorious
  world.

~

Raining leaves
Leaves sigh,
whisper,
glide
and flop to the ground.
Thank you, Lord, for the surprising
and quiet sounds of the world.

~

Autumn is a lovely season
There are dark, bright, shining conkers
  on the ground,
in the hedgerows red berries glow like
  fire,

47

~

in the orchards fruit has ripened and is
  gathered, gently,
in the barns the golden wheat is stored.
For all the colours and beauties of
  autumn
we praise your name,
most holy and most loving God.

~

Snow
The snow has blanketed the world with
a rare and lovely softness. We praise
you, God, for the pure white beauty of
snow.

~

Crisp, clear mornings
The sky is an icy blue, the hedges are
  edged with silver,
the sun bounces light around
  everything . . .
Thank you, God, for the unexpected
  brilliance of a lovely day.

~

Moonlight
Soft, pale moonlight bathes the world
— and all is very, very quiet.
  God, let your peace be in our minds
as softly as the moonlight.

Winter thaw
Thaw my soul with the warmth of
 your love, O God,
for I feel cold, and hard and bitter;
I long for the signs of your spring in
 me,
when I can come alive with joy.

∼

Snowdrops
Like tiny nuns bobbing in a church, the
snowdrops dance in the wind. Thank
you, God, for the delicate promise of
spring and new life.

∼

Yellow
Yellow daffodils . . .
Like fragile stars, like a captured
 sunbeam,
the daffodils dance in the breeze.
Lord, for the gold of bright new life,
we praise your name, O God.

∼

Laughter in the street
The sun's shining; it's a blue-sky day
 and in the street
people are talking and smiling and
 laughing.
For loud voices, soft voices,
For kind voices, gentle voices,
For peals of laughter and silent smiles,
we thank you, heavenly Father.

49

∼

Pippa's song

The year's at the spring,
And day's at the morn;
Morning's at seven;
The hill-side's dew-pearled;
The lark's on the wing;
The snail's on the thorn:
God's in his heaven —
All's right with the world!

ROBERT BROWNING

~

Grasshoppers

The grasshoppers click and whirr like
tiny green machines lost in a miniature
jungle . . .

As grasshoppers signal across their
world, so we signal our praise to you,
O God of the universe.

~

Summer Days

The sky is a pure deep blue,
the breeze is rustling the leaves,
bees buzz drowsily around the flowers.
In the next door garden
I can hear the whirr of a lawn mower.
O God, on warm and sunny summer
    days
I am glad to be alive.
Thank you.

Seaside
For buckets and spades, for sunshine
    and shade,
For sand in the toes, for cream on the
    nose,
For jumping the tide, for having a ride,
For laughter and fun, praise God every
    one.

~

Turquoise and purple
When the sun is setting and the sky
changes colour very, very slowly and
with great beauty, accept our quiet joy
as our thanksgiving to you, O Lord
our God.

~

What a wonderful world!
To see a World in a Grain of Sand,
And a Heaven in a Wild Flower,
Hold Infinity in the palm of your hand
And Eternity in an hour.

WILLIAM BLAKE

~

The skylark
I couldn't see the skylark — he was too
    high up in the sky for that — but I
    could hear him.
Music from nowhere, music for the
    sheer joy of it.
Make us, Lord, as happy as skylarks.

51
~

Sounds

God has given us on this earth a kind
  of living orchestra:
the soft and gentle sound of water in a
  brook,
the rolling drums of thunder,
the pure beauty of bird song.
Keep our ears open to the hidden music
  in our world,
so that we may praise you for its
  loveliness,
now and always.

≈

Morning

Morning has broken like the first
  morning,
Blackbirds have spoken like the first
  bird.
Praise for the singing! praise for the
  morning!
Praise for them springing, fresh from
  the word!

ELEANOR FARJEON

≈

Listening to music

Father in heaven, I bless you for those
  who make music.
May I listen to music with such joyful
  attention
that my life may become a song of
  praise.

≈

Families

Families

There are many kinds of families in the world. Some have mothers and fathers and children; some have just mothers and children; others just fathers and children. Some have grandparents or step-grandparents, others do not have grandparents at all. Some have dozens of cousins in the family, others have none. And some people set up special kinds of families: in schools and communities, or as monks and nuns.

Whatever kind of family we live in, we human beings are at our best with other people. We can't live totally isolated lives and depend on no one. Even hermits have their memories of families.

But we not only belong to our own local family, we also belong to the world family: all those other children and parents and grandparents and cousins and uncles and aunts. All of us share a common inheritance and need to learn to live peaceably in the world village.

Christians believe that they also belong to a kind of 'invisible' family: the family of those who believe in Jesus, whether alive now or dead. This family is sometimes called 'the communion of saints' and extends from heaven to earth.

Prayer is a way of discovering the variety of families to which we belong – and praising God, the parent of us all.

Jesus' mother and brothers came to him, but were unable to join him because of the crowd. Someone said to Jesus, 'Your mother and brothers are standing outside and want to see you.'

Jesus said to them all, 'My mother and brothers are those who hear the word of God and obey it.'

LUKE 8:19–21

~

Jesus at home

Jesus, Lord and brother,
at Nazareth you grew to manhood
busy in the sunlit workshop with eye
    and hand and brain,
yet ever dreaming of a kingdom to be
    built,
world-wide, eternal, not made with
    hands:
Help us to grow in wisdom, loving the
    things of heaven,
seeing the world, as with your eyes, at
    its true value,
for the sake of yourself, our Saviour
    Jesus Christ.

SHORT PRAYERS FOR THE LONG DAY,
GILES AND MELVILLE HARCOURT

~

Parents

Lord, I remember my parents,
my brothers and sisters.
My day was easy.
My arms are not swollen,
my back does not hurt.
Lord,
I was sitting on a stool
while father dug in the ground.
I drew the lines on the paper
while mother prepared the meals
and everybody busied himself for me.

Lord,
keep my parents in your love.
Lord,
bless them and keep them.
Lord,
please let me have money and strength
and keep my parents for many more
 years
so that I can take care of them.

PRAYER OF A YOUNG GHANAIAN CHRISTIAN

~

Families

Bless, O God, our families. Give to
those who care for us the spirit of
understanding and the spirit of love,
that our homes may be places of peace
and of laughter; for Jesus' sake.

~

Family peace
Come into our homes, O Lord, and
protect us with your love, so that we
may live in peace and rejoice in the
quiet beauty of your blessing.

∼

Father-and-Mother God
There are some things, O Lord,
which are very difficult to put into
    words;
like the times when I am happy,
like the times when I know
how much my parents care for me;
I want to let them know
how much I care for them,
that I will do anything I can
to help them in their lives.
As I thank you for them,
I realize that you, O Lord, are
like a Father and a Mother
to everyone,
to my parents,
to me,
to the world
and my thanks for that are beyond all
    words.

∼

Parents, when anxious
Direct with your loving kindness our
    parents, O God.
When they are tired, strengthen them;

58

∼

When they are worried, sustain them;
When the are bewildered, encourage
    them;
and in all their fears give them your
    hope
and peace that their lives may be
    renewed
today, tomorrow and for ever.

~

God bless
God bless all those that I love;
God bless all those that love me;
God bless all those that love those that
    I love,
And all those that love those that love
    me.

ANON

~

Grannies and grandads
The great thing about grannies and
    grandads
is that they have time for us,
and they're not cross,
and they're good people to be with.
O God, bless them with your love
and let them know that we love and
    appreciate them
very much.

~

Nannas and Poppas

They have wrinkly faces
but very kind eyes;
they have stories to tell us
and surprises to share;
they are very beautiful to us, O God,
thank you for them.

~

Grandparents

Let the warmth and kindness of your
love, O Lord,
surround our grandparents
that they may be safe and at peace,
today and for always.

~

Cherishing grandparents

Thank you, Father, for our
    grandparents.
Teach us to be thankful for their
kindness,
and as they grow older, may we
cherish them like they cherish us.

~

Brothers and sisters

Holy Father, heavenly king, let your
blessing rest upon our brothers and
sisters and all our family. May our lives
together be touched by the strength and
the laughter of heaven.

~

God of all the families
You are the God of all the families
upon this earth,
you are to us all like a mother,
like a father,
teach us in your gentle power
how we may live together in unity
and peace
now and for ever.

∼

Promises
Now another day is breaking,
Sleep was sweet and so is waking,
Dear Lord, I promised you last night
Never again to sulk or fight.
Such vows are easier to keep
When a child is sound asleep.
Today, O Lord, for your dear sake,
I'll try to keep them when awake.

OGDEN NASH

∼

A new brother or sister
Blessed Lord in heaven,
today I am so excited
I can hardly breathe,
because a new baby
is coming to our home.
Help me to share my happiness with
my whole family,
so that we can all be close
to your love in our new life together.

61

∼

Baby coming home
Dear God, I'm very excited
because today my new baby
    brother/sister
will come home from hospital.
Help me to be helpful
and to understand all that he/she needs.

~

Bless our new baby
Lord God, you were born as a baby in
    a stable,
bless my new sister/brother with your
    love and strength.
As she/he grows up help us to enjoy
    our lives together.

~

Aunties and uncles
O God, bless my aunts,
O God, bless my uncles,
O God, bless my cousins,
and all of my family,
that we may reflect your happiness
in our lives one with another.

~

Foster-parents
Dearest God, I know I can tell you
    everything;
I am glad to be here, safe and sound,
even though sometimes I am
    bewildered and sad;
let your peace and strength rest on all
    of us
so that with your love we may grow
in our understanding of one another
    and of you.

                    ~

God like a parent
I look around
at all the faces of the children
in my school
and see that some are happy,
some are sad,
some are frightened
some are full of fun,
and I know that You
are like a parent to us all;
You have promised that You will
always be with us,
however we feel,
wherever we are,
for You are the father or mother of
everyone
and will never let us down.

Step-parents
Lord God, when new people come to
live in our home, may they be patient
and very, very kind and think of us as
well as themselves.

~

Prayer for a new parent
Dearest God,
you know that I now have a new
    mummy/daddy.
It's going to take me a while
to get used to things
and, to be honest,
calling them 'Mum/Dad'
is very, very hard . . .
so hard that I want to cry . . .
Please help me to understand myself
so that I can gradually be at peace —
    with them,
with me, and with you.

~

Care for the elderly
Be with all those, O Lord, who care
    for the old;
give them patience and strength,
    gentleness and love,
that the dignity of all may be
    maintained,
for Jesus Christ's sake.

~

Looking back over life
Enlarge our minds to appreciate the past,
deepen our hearts to understand the
    present,
open our eyes to see your love, O God,
now and for ever.

 ～

Our own attitudes to the elderly
O God, help us to see and appreciate
the gifts of the elderly,
their wisdom and their experience;
and bring all generations closer
    together,
that we may understand and
love one another.

 ～

Old people
There are some old people whose lives
are like autumn, mellow, quiet and
    wise.
Help us, Lord, to admire them
and to listen to them patiently.

 ～

Unhappy families
O God, you are the only one we can
    turn to:
please, please bring kindness and peace
    back to our homes,
for we need you very much;
and help us to understand what is
    going on.

 ～

Family strife
Dearest God, my parents upset me
with their rows and quarrels,
and I hate it when they shout at each
    other.
I bring this to you for I need you now
more than ever.
God — be my friend.

~

Family strife
Dearest God, please listen to me,
I am sad and angry and frightened
because my parents keep having rows.
They shriek at each other
and their faces become ugly.
When this happens, please be very close
    to me
and to them,
and help them to learn to love and care
    for each other
like they used to do.

~

On the death of a grandparent
Dear God, I don't know how to say
what I want to say;
My gran (dad) has died
and I miss her (him) very much.
She/he had such a smiling face
and a twinkling eye,
and was very kind to me.
I remember her/his hands,

66

~

the clothes she/he wore
and the way she/he always had time for
    me.
Thank you for her/him and please take
    care of her/him
in heaven until we see each other again.

On the death of someone we love
Lord in heaven, you have promised us
new life through your Son, Jesus
Christ; help us to live with that
promise in our hearts and in our lives,
so that our sadness can be turned by
you into blessing and strength in the
days ahead.

Tears
Almighty God, Father of all mankind,
in your Son you took upon yourself
the world's sorrow.
We offer you our own sorrow and
    sadness,
knowing that you can help us to bear
    our grief
through the infinite understanding and
    love of Jesus Christ our Lord.

Our hope and strength
Lord, you are our hope and strength,
strong as a rock,
gentle as a dove.
Comfort with your kindly power
all those who are torn apart by grief.
Even in their darkness and despair
may they find you,
and know that you cherish them
in all things, and will bring them hope.

Friends

Friends

When Jesus lived on earth he chose a number of people to be his special friends. We call them 'the disciples'. He called them 'friends'.

In our lives we too need friends and as we grow up we learn how to make friends. Friendship is one of the greatest blessings of life: the shared laughter; the shared games; the shared experiences.

You know how lovely it is to have friends and to be a friend. Think how much more lovely it is to know that God loves us like a true friend. He shares all that we go through. He is happy when we are happy, and helps us to bear our sadness when we are sad.

And God has broken the power of death, so that when we die we can continue our friendship with him for ever.

Prayer is a way of letting God be our friend, and strengthening our friendship with others.

'My commandment is this: love one another just as I love you. The greatest love a person can have for his friends is to give his life for them. And you are my friends if you do what I command you. I do not call you servants any longer, because a servant does not know what his master is doing. Instead, I call you friends, because I have told you everything I have heard from my Father. You did not choose me; I chose you and appointed you to go and bear much fruit, the kind of fruit that endures. And so the Father will give you whatever you ask of him in my name. This, then, is what I command you: love one another.

JOHN 15:12–17

~

Loyalty

Grant us, O Lord, loyalty of heart, so that as we expect others to be faithful to us, we also may be faithful to them; for Jesus Christ's sake.

~

Friends far away

O Lord, we bring to you our friends . . . who live far away. May they be aware of your blessing upon them, and grant that although we are separated from them by great distances, we may be aware of your love uniting us. This we ask for Jesus' sake.

~

Strong friendships
Let our friendships be so strong,
  O Lord,
that they become a blessing to others.
Let our friendships be so open,
  O Lord,
that they may be a haven for others.
Let our friendships be so gentle,
  O Lord,
that they may bring peace to others.

~

God loves me
I am held
in the arms of God;
I am safe
in the hands of God;
I am kept
in the mind of God;
God loves me now and always.

~

Thank you for friends
There are huggy friends,
noisy friends,
quiet friends,
laughing friends —
for all my friends who love me,
for all those friends whom I love,
I bless you, heavenly Father.

~

Being friends
O Lord,
you are the friend of us all,
help me to show in my friendship for
  others,
the kind of love you have for me.

༄

Feeling lonely
I feel lonely today. Everyone else seems
to have friends, but I don't. Help me to
know that you, God, are a friend to
everyone, and that you are the greatest
friend any of us could ever hope for.

༄

Loneliness
Dear Lord,
When I am sad and alone
I pray to you and then
I am not lonely anymore.

༄

Saying 'No'
Dear Lord,
my friend keeps asking me to do things
that I don't want to do,
but I can't say 'No' to her.
Please help me to say 'No' to things.

༄

Secrets

Oh, the joy of telling secrets,
of sharing special stories
special jokes
special fears.
But keep me wise, O God,
and keep me honest,
that I may be trustworthy
and true; for others and for you.

~

Betrayal

Father God,
I thought I could trust my friends.
I told them everything,
shared secrets, told jokes,
and now they are telling the whole
  world
and are laughing at me . . .
and it leaves me feeling hollow
and bitter and sad inside.
Help me to understand my feelings
and my friends,
that I may grow in strength and
  confidence
and be trustworthy for others
now and always.

~

Quarrelling and making up

O God, you have taught us that
we can come to you and say 'sorry'
and that you will forgive us;
Give me the courage and the grace
to accept other people when they say
that they are sorry
so that our friendships can be mended
and go from strength to strength.

～

New and unexpected friends

Lord God, when today began
it was clean and new and fresh
and I had no idea that I would make a
    new friend;
I am so happy
that all the cleanness and newness and
    freshness
seem to be inside me and I'm
looking forward with laughter
to meeting my new friend tomorrow.

～

The friendship of God

Lord, the stars float from Thy hands
like silver bubbles.
The clouds wrap themselves around
    Thy fingers.
Rivers flow across Thy palms which are
    covered
with miles of forest and green fields
    and lakes

that have formed in their hollows.
Suns flash from Thy forehead.
Universes dance about Thy feet . . .

And yet, O Lord,
Thou didst tread the dusty road
that led to Golgotha.
Thou didst hang upon a cruel cross
for love of mere men.

CHANDRAN DEVANESEN: *ANOTHER DAY*, CARDEN

School

School

As we grow up we learn more and more. We learn more about ourselves, about other people, about the world. Learning never really stops – not even when we are grown up.

We begin our learning at home with those who care for us. And then we move perhaps to a nursery school, and one day we go to school.

The first day at school is often memorable. (Can you remember what happened?) There are so many new faces, new places, new names. But as the days pass the newness wears off and we look back and wonder why we felt so worried.

God seems to have made us with an unlimited capacity to learn and adapt. He trusts us to care for the world and to share in its development. Jesus came to the world as a Teacher to help us learn the truth about ourselves and God.

Prayer is a way of learning more about God and of discovering how God wants us to share in the way the world develops.

Jesus saw the crowds who were there. He went up on a hill and sat down. His followers came to him. Jesus taught the people and said:

'Those who know they have great
   spiritual needs are happy.
The kingdom of heaven belongs to
   them.
Those who are sad now are happy.
God will comfort them.
Those who are humble are happy.
The earth will belong to them.
Those who want to do right more than
   anything else are happy.
God will satisfy them.
Those who give mercy to others are
   happy.
Mercy will be given to them.
Those who are pure in their thinking
   are happy.
They will be with God.
Those who work to bring peace are
   happy.
God will call them his sons.
Those who are treated badly for doing
   good are happy.
The kingdom of heaven belongs to
   them.'

MATTHEW 5:1–10

82

God in our school
Lord, let your Holy Spirit rest upon
  our school
that it may be a place of love and truth
where the weak are made strong
and the strong learn humility
and all of us learn the wisdom
that alone comes from you.

God bless our school
God bless our school:
bless those who teach
bless those who learn
and bless us all with the knowledge of
  your love
through Jesus Christ our Lord.

A new school
It will be so new,
new desks,
new chairs,
new books,
new teachers,
new children . . .
Let me be aware that you wait for me
in the newness, O Lord,
and will give me the strength and peace
  I need.

For those who have no school
O Lord and heavenly Father,
we bring to you in our prayers
those children who have no schools
and no opportunity to learn;
may we be generous in caring for them
and share with them our learning and
　our wealth,
for all good things are given to us to
　share.

～

Blessing on a school
Let thy blessing, O Lord, rest upon our
work in this school. Teach us to seek
after the truth and enable us to attain it.
But grant that as we increase in
knowledge of earthly things, we may
grow in knowledge of thee, whom to
know is life eternal; through Jesus
Christ our Lord.

ADAPTED FROM THOMAS ARNOLD

～

Open our eyes to truth
Holy and loving God,
open our eyes to see you,
open our minds to trust you,
open our hearts to love you,
this day and for evermore.

Books
We thank you, Father, for the authors
  and books
which have given us the greatest
  pleasure.
We remember their names before you
  now . . . .
Help us to use words wisely and well,
expressing our thoughts in a clear and
  truthful way.

~

Fair play
O God, look upon our school with
  love,
that it may be a place of hope for the
  fearful,
a refuge for the despised,
and a protection for the weak.
Above all make it a place
where truth may flourish
and fair dealing abound
and life be lived to the full.

~

Circle of friends
A circle can be so strong and
forbidding. It's fine for those inside, but
for those outside it's not so good. May
our circles of friends always be open to
the needs of others, so that we may be
generous and not mean, thoughtful and
not spiteful, for Jesus' sake.

85
~

Thankfulness for friends

Lord God, thank you for all my friends,
for the jokes we share,
the games we play,
and the work we do together.

～

Difficulties in friendships

Today, God, I got so angry.
There were my friends,
who kept calling me names
and teasing and whispering.
It was horrible, and they wouldn't let
me play with them.
Give me, please, the sense of humour
and the courage, I need
to understand them,
and to understand myself,
so that I can be friends with them
again.

～

Those without friends

They always seem to stand alone,
over by the wall in the playground,
and when anyone speaks they just grunt
or don't reply,
and their eyes look so unhappy:
O God, let them know that you love
them
and that trusting in you
they can gradually learn to trust others,
for Jesus' sake.

～

Living for God

Lord, may I be wakeful at sunrise to begin a new day for Thee; cheerful at sunset for having done my work for Thee; thankful at moonrise and under starshine for the beauty of Thy universe. And may I add what little may be in me to Thy great world.

THE ABBOT OF GREVE: *ANOTHER DAY*, CARDEN

~

Generosity

Dear God, make us generous in body,
   mind and soul,
that in giving ourselves in love for
   others
we may give ourselves to you.

~

Help us to love

Most glorious God,
your love beats at the heart of the
   world;
make our hearts generous with love
that we may share in your yearning
for the peace and healing of all.

~

My teachers

Dear God,
I should like to tell you about my
   teachers:
there's one who always seems cross and
   I'm a bit afraid of him;

87

~

there's one who is kind and I like her;
there's one who has taught me how to
  draw
and that makes me very happy.
Bless them all, O God, the cross, the
  kind, the helpful,
and teach us how to use our gifts for
  others.

~

Bless our teachers
Lord God and heavenly Father,
you sent your Son Jesus to live among
  us
that we might learn of you;
let the Spirit of Jesus rest upon our
  teachers
that they may be wise and truthful,
  loving and good
in all they think and speak and do.

~

Success and failure
Lord God,
in Jesus you showed us that real
  greatness
lies in service;
help us to use our success
for the well-being of others
and for the glory of your name.

~

Life out of darkness
Dear Father God,
in the death of Jesus
you transformed failure into victory
and brought new life out of the
   darkness;
please help me in my failures
to see the promise of new life
and to live as courageously as he did.

Exams
Today, dear Lord, I have an exam.
Can you imagine how I feel? —
a bit afraid,
a bit excited . . .
but I shall need your quiet love
deep inside my heart and mind
to help me.
Thank you for being with me
now and always.

Passing an exam
I should like to do a handstand,
a cartwheel,
run as fast as the wind,
fly like an eagle,
because I've passed my exam.
In my joy, O Lord, I give you thanks
and pray that my new achievement
will be for your glory and for the good
   of others.

Failing an exam
It's no good, O God;
I've failed again.
I knew it. I knew it as soon as my
    name was called.
That same sinking feeling in the
    stomach,
the pointlessness,
the hopelessness.
I've failed . . .

God replies:
Ah, but my child,
You are never a failure
in my eyes.
I cherish you with my love,
and through your sorrow
will strengthen and uphold you
today and for ever,
and reveal gifts that will surprise you.

⟡

Not being chosen
O God,
I hate the humiliation of not being
    chosen.
I stand on my own when the teams are
    being picked
and I hear their comments: 'He can't
    catch';
'She can't run' . . .
It's awful.

90
⟡

Can't they understand how I feel,
  always being left out?
Show me please the way to cope
so that I can keep a sense of humour
and learn that in failure
there are always doorways
to new opportunities.

❧

Winning

The cheers,
the applause.
Basking in delight . .
Thank you for the joy of winning,
but help me to remain humble, Lord,
and to keep a sense of humour.

❧

Losing

So there we are, God . . .
I'm getting used to losing
and I do not like it.
I do not like it one little bit.
Please help me when I lose
to pick myself up
and try again
so that I learn courage and hope
and perseverance.

❧

Bullies

Father in heaven, please let your love
  work
within the hearts of those who bully,
that they may cease from their cruelty
and learn to be at peace with themselves
and with others.

~

Unkindness

O Lord Jesus, we confess that we are
  sometimes
deliberately unkind to other people.
  Forgive us and help us to show them
  your love.

~

Jesus and his friends

Lord Jesus,
you chose twelve people
to be your special and closest friends;
they were with you wherever you went,
saw your miracles,
saw the healings;
yet when you most needed them
they ran away, frightened.
Even so, you forgave them,
brought them new life
and courageously they told the world
about you.
Thank you Jesus for those friends,
who have brought us the good news of
  God.

~

Fear
O God, I hate being afraid; there's a
fluttering in my stomach and my legs
feel like jelly. I want to run away and
hide. Show me the way through, O
God, and may your promise to be with
me make me strong.

≈

Discipline
Help me, O Lord, to learn
that no new skill is mastered
without attention and hard work.
Give me the grace when the
    breakthrough comes
to rejoice wholeheartedly
and dedicate my new skills
to my neighbours and to you.

≈

New subjects
Here it comes, O Lord,
the brand new book with crisp white
    pages . . .
As I learn (with that mixture of
    excitement and fear)
keep me thankful and open-hearted
to the boundless surprises of your
    world.

People who look after us

People who look after us

Look around your room. See that window? Someone made it in a factory. See that light bulb? Someone made that. See that carpet? Someone made it.

Everything we have has been created by the energy and determination and hard work of people we have never met.

The more you look around, the more you realise that we depend on other people. Jesus said we all have one Father in heaven – and if we have one Father, then that means everyone is our sister and our brother.

Prayer is a way of thanking God for making us part of the world family.

During this time a man from the tribe of Levi married a woman of his own tribe, and she bore him a son. When she saw what a fine baby he was, she hid him for three months. But when she could not hide him any longer, she took a basket made of reeds and covered it with tar to make it watertight. She put the baby in it and then placed it in the tall grass at the edge of the river. The baby's sister stood some distance away to see what would happen to him.

The king's daughter came down to the river to bathe, while her servants walked along the bank. Suddenly she noticed the basket in the tall grass and sent a slave-girl to get it. The princess opened it and saw a baby boy. He was crying, and she felt sorry for him. 'This is one of the Hebrew babies,' she said.

Then his sister asked her, 'Shall I go and call a Hebrew woman to act as a wet-nurse?'

'Please do,' she answered. So the girl went and brought the baby's own mother. The princess told the woman, 'Take this baby and nurse him for me, and I will pay you.' So she took the baby and nursed him. Later, when the child was old enough, she took him to the king's daughter, who adopted him as her own son. She said to herself, 'I pulled him out of the water, and so I name him Moses.'

When Moses had grown up, he went out to visit his people, the Hebrews, and he saw how they were forced to do hard labour. He even saw an Egyptian kill a Hebrew, one of Moses' own people. Moses looked all round, and when he saw that no one was watching, he killed the Egyptian and hid his body in the sand.

The next day he went back and saw two Hebrew men fighting. He said to the one who was in the wrong, 'Why are you beating up a fellow-Hebrew?'

The man answered, 'Who made you our ruler and judge? Are you going to kill me just as you killed that Egyptian?' Then Moses was afraid and said to himself, 'People have found out what I have done.' When the king heard about what had happened, he tried to have Moses killed, but Moses fled and went to live in the land of Midian.

One day, when Moses was sitting by a well, seven daughters of Jethro, the priest of Midian, came to draw water and fill the troughs of their father's sheep and goats. But some shepherds drove Jethro's daughters away. Then Moses went to their rescue and watered their animals for them. When they returned to their father, he asked, 'Why have you come back so early today?'

'An Egyptian rescued us from the shepherds,' they answered, 'and he even drew water for us and watered our animals.'

'Where is he?' he asked his daughters. 'Why did you leave the man out there? Go and invite him to eat with us.'

So Moses agreed to live there, and

Jethro gave him his daughter Zipporah in marriage, who bore him a son. Moses said to himself, 'I am a foreigner in this land, and so I name him Gershom.'

Years later the king of Egypt died, but the Israelites were still groaning under their slavery and cried out for help. Their cry went up to God, who heard their groaning and remembered his covenant with Abraham, Isaac and Jacob. He saw the slavery of the Israelites and was concerned for them.

EXODUS 2:1–25

∾

Police

O holy God and heavenly Father,
bless with your wisdom all those
   people who uphold the law.
When they are perplexed, guide them;
when they are in danger, protect them;
when they are exhausted, uphold them;
that they may be people of integrity
   and truth,
working with us all
for a better society.

Firemen
The first thing I heard was the siren
    wailing,
(dee-dah, dee-dah, dee-dah)
and then I saw the fire-engine roaring
    past
rushing to put out a fire.
O God, thank you for all those
who risk their lives for others,
surround them with your love and care
and keep them safe in all their dangers.

⁓

For all who help
Here's a kind of list, O God,
let me read it to you:
doctors, nurses, teachers, clergy,
    ambulance crew, paramedics, cleaners
    . . . and there are lots more,
all those people who help others.
Thank you, God, for them all.

⁓

Doctors and nurses
O God, the giver of life and health and
joy, we pray that your will may be
done in and for those who suffer
sickness or disease. Through the
ministry of men and women who have
understanding and ability to help, may
they be restored to soundness of body
and mind; and through medical research
and discovery may new cures be found

101

⁓

to bring fresh hope to the world;
through Jesus Christ our Lord.
PRAYERS FOR USE AT ALTERNATIVE SERVICES

~

Eye surgeons

Give to all eye surgeons, O Lord,
skill, compassion and tenderness,
that all who come into their care may
　see
your gifts at work in the world.

~

Technology for deaf people

Dear God, your skill is infinite; give to
all scientists and technicians the
patience and the wisdom, the love and
the dedication to create new ways for
deaf people to hear; so that we all may
grow in understanding of you and of
each other. This we ask for Jesus' sake.

~

Speech therapists

Lord Jesus, Word of God, you
　proclaimed your love in story
and brought healing through your
　speech;
bless all speech therapists
that they may be patient and skilful in
　their work
and bring to those who suffer
your word of peace and love.

~

Physiotherapists
Lord Jesus, you laid your hands on
those who were ill and brought them to
peace and healing; pour your healing gifts
upon all physiotherapists, that they may
bring solace and strength to all in need.

~

Shopkeepers
Let your blessing rest softly upon those
who serve us in shops,
and may we treat them with gratitude
and courtesy for their service to us and
    to others,
for Jesus' sake, the Servant of all.

~

Farmers
Lord of seed-time and harvest,
grant to those who farm,
the skill to grow good food,
and such wisdom in the use of the land
that it may be fruitful for the
    generations yet to come.

~

Seafarers
Almighty and eternal God, whose way
    is on the deep,
We commend to thy fatherly care, all
    that go down to the sea in ships and
    occupy their business in great waters.
Help them in whatever lies before
    them, to quit themselves like men.

103

~

If there be any duty may they do it
with cheerfulness.
If any danger, may they face it with
courage,
Knowing thy hand is in all things
and all things are in thy hand.
We ask it for thy Name's sake.

DAILY PRAYERS, BRIGGS & MILNER–WHITE

~

Lifeboatmen

Thank you, heavenly Father, for those
who risk their lives in storms and great
dangers to bring others to safety.

When they are frightened, protect
them; when they are in peril, comfort
them; and give them at all times, your
peace and your strength, for Jesus' sake.

~

Merchant and Royal Navies

Father, when Jesus lived in Palestine, he
brought peace to the storm on the lake.
May he also bring his peace to those
who spend their lives on the oceans of
the world, that they may be aware of
his presence every day.

~

Industry

Father, thank you for all the good
things made in factories. May we never
be so carefree in the use of things that
we forget the toil that has gone into
making them.

∼

Dustmen

Dear God, may those who sweep and
    clean
and take away our rubbish
be assured of your love and our respect
for you are the servant of all.

∼

Water supply

The water gushes through our taps; it
fills our baths; it provides our drinks; it
refreshes us deeply . . .

    O Lord, bless the bringers of water,
that they may rejoice in the bounty of
the earth, and turn to you, their living
water, for the refreshment of their
souls.

365 PRAYERS

∼

Electricity and gas

Your energy, O God, is let loose in the
    world
bringing us life and joy and pleasure.
Bless those whose lives are devoted to
    the energies of creation,

105

∼

that in their work they may feel you
   very near,
and be aware of your unending love for
   them and for everyone.

∽

Offering of work to God
As tools come to be sharpened by the
blacksmith, so may we come, O Lord.
As sharpened tools go back with their
owner, so may we go back to our
everyday life and work, to be used by
thee, O Lord.

MORNING, NOON & NIGHT

∽

People at work
Lord, I pray for my poor father.
He works so hard and tries so hard to
   help
my mother and us the children.
But his salary is so small he cannot do
   all
the things he wants to do for us.
Help us to be good children who love
   him,
and who encourage him
to keep his trust in you.
Some day, we believe,
everything will be all right.

MORNING, NOON & NIGHT

∽

The postman

If the postman has parcels he rings or
  knocks,
Letters and postcards he drops in the
  box.
The postman's my friend, and a friend
  of mine
Is the boy with the papers who comes
  before nine.
There's that man with a book who
  reads the meter,
The coalman, the milkman, the window
  cleaner.
They're all busy people who work hard
  all day,
So bless them, dear Lord, as they go on
  their way.

HELLO GOD, WINN

~

Night workers

I'm thinking of the engine drivers,
Driving through the night.
Policemen on their lonely beat,
Firemen with fires to fight.
Doctors, nurses, factory workers.
Be with them, dear Lord,
While most of us are sleeping,
They are working hard.

HELLO GOD, WINN

~

Guide our rulers

I am baffled, O God, by the world.
Why can't the politicians bring peace?
Why can't people stop killing each
    other?
Why can't everyone live together in
    harmony?
More questions than prayers, O God —
but perhaps my questions are my
    prayers?

～

Make our rulers wise and good

Dear Lord and heavenly Father,
make the rulers of our land wise and
    good;
that in wisdom they may work for
    truth
and in goodness they may care for the
    poor;
this we ask in Jesus' name.

～

Give rulers wisdom

Dear Father in heaven,
let the wisdom of your Holy Spirit
guide the hearts and minds of our
    rulers,
that they may speak the truth,
act with justice,
and humbly acknowledge the worth of
    all;
for Jesus' sake.

108

～

Special days

Special days

You know how exciting it is waiting for the postman to call when it's your birthday. You wake early, look out of the window to see if he's coming down the road, creep downstairs to see if he came early. And there's nothing there. So you wait. Or rather, you wait by dashing around picking things up, putting them down, talking more loudly than usual, laughing – and then the door bell rings . . .

Perhaps you remember the excitement of preparing to go on holiday. (What shall I wear? Shall I pack my favourite toy?) Or you may know the excitement of going to see a friend.

As well as special days of happiness, there are also special days when you are feeling a bit nervous, like starting a new school, or taking an exam.

Whatever kind of day it is, every day is God's day. He is there in the excitement. He is there in the anxiety, bringing you new understanding, helping you to cope with the newness of things.

Prayer is a way of putting God at the living centre of every day – so that each day is hallowed and blessed.

Every year the parents of Jesus went to Jerusalem for the Passover Festival. When Jesus was twelve years old, they went to the festival as usual. When the festival was over, they started back home, but the boy Jesus stayed in Jerusalem. His parents did not know this; they thought that he was with the group, so they travelled a whole day and then started looking for him among their relatives and friends. They did not find him, so they went back to Jerusalem looking for him. On the third day they found him in the Temple, sitting with the Jewish teachers, listening to them and asking questions. All who heard him were amazed at his intelligent answers. His parents were astonished when they saw him, and his mother said to him, 'My son, why have you done this to us? Your father and I have been terribly worried trying to find you.'

He answered them, 'Why did you have to look for me? Didn't you know that I had to be in my Father's house?' But they did not understand his answer.

So Jesus went back with them to Nazareth, where he was obedient to them. His mother treasured all these things in her heart. Jesus grew both in body and in wisdom, gaining favour with God and men.

LUKE 2:41–52

My birthday

My heavenly Father, all last year you
    took care of me,
And now you have given me a
    birthday.
I thank you for all your goodness and
    kindness to me.
You have given me loving parents, a
    home, gifts and clothes.
Help me to be a better child in the
    coming year . . .
To grow strong, to study well and to
    work happily.

HELLO GOD, WINN

❧

A new year

The door of my last year is closing,
the door of my new year is opening.
Wherever I go,
whatever I do,
walk with me, Lord,
that I may live with thanksgiving in
    my heart
and love in all that I do;
for Jesus' sake.

A new beginning
Father, you have brought me to the
   beginning of another year in my life;
I bless you for those who have given
   me birth,
I bless you for those who care for me
   now, and I bless you for the year
   ahead.

~

Birthday blessing
Every day is someone's birthday, Lord.
Today I am thinking of . . . .
Help me to make it a very special day
In every possible kind of way.
And may your ever-loving care
Keep . . . . safe throughout the year.

~

Collecting the Christmas tree
Dearest God, may this tree, strong and
green and lovely, be a sign to us of
your everlasting love and your joy in
our world.

~

Decorating the Christmas tree
These are the things we love:
the tinsel glinting . . .
the lights in the branches . . .
the bauble turning very, very slowly . . .
Lord, thank you for the deep, deep
   promise of Christmas.

114

~

The Bethlehem shepherds
If only we could have been there, Lord,
on that hillside. We should have heard
the sheep baa-ing, the dogs barking,
the silence of the night — and then,
stars-full of your glory and the sounds
of peace and goodwill . . .
'Glory to God in the highest . . .'

The shepherds at the manger
Father, as those first shepherds knelt at
the cradle, may we kneel quietly before
you just because we love you — our
God and our King.

Sharing the songs of angels
O God, our loving Father, help us
rightly to remember the birth of Jesus,
that we may share in the songs of the
angels, the gladness of the shepherds,
and the worship of the wise men. May
the Christmas morning make us happy
to be your children, and the Christmas
evenings bring us to our beds with
grateful thoughts, forgiving and
forgiven, for Jesus' sake.

PUFFIN BOOK OF PRAYERS, R.L. STEVENSON

The Holy Baby

On this special day, O Lord,
we remember your birth as a baby;
in a manger lying on straw,
the cattle and donkey close by,
and Mary and Joseph looking upon you
with amazed and holy love.
We bless you for coming among us
as a child
and pray that the joy of this day
may bring peace and hope to all the
world.

～

The Nativity

Dear Master,
May Thy light
Shine on me now,
As once it shone
Upon the shepherds,
As they kept their flocks
By night.

MORNING, NOON & NIGHT

～

Too busy for Christ

Let not our souls be busy inns that
   have no room for Thee and Thine,
   but quiet homes of prayer and praise
   where Thou mayest find fit company;
   where the needful cares of life are
   wisely ordered and put away, and
   wide sweet spaces kept for Thee;

116

～

where holy thoughts pass up and
   down, and fervent longings watch
   and wait Thy coming.

MORNING, NOON & NIGHT

~

Bless the lonely

I can hardly bear to think about it, O
   God,
all those people who are very lonely,
who feel left out,
who have no one to turn to.
At Christmas time they must feel sadder
and lonelier than ever.
Help them in their loneliness
to discover that you are always with
   them
and will lead them towards happiness
and new life.

~

The manger

The hard wood of the manger
was softened by golden straw
so that you had a place to lay your
   head,
Lord Jesus.
Soften with your gentle love
all the hard places of the world,
so that those who live there
may learn your peace
and your most humble love.

~

The happiness of Christmas
There are fat, squashy presents,
long, thin, bending presents,
presents which are huge,
presents which are very small.
Amongst all the excitement of guessing,
let us never forget, O Lord,
that you came among us
as the gift of God himself
to heal our broken world.

～

Coming to the stable
Lowly we bend the knee,
Humbly we worship thee,
Lord Jesus, set us free
to live in peace.

～

Room at the inn
Almighty God, full of mercy, look
down with pity upon all the innkeepers
of the world who turn guests away
because of their colour or creed or
condition. Prepare room in our hearts,
that those who are hurt or rejected or
ignored in the world may find kindness
there. In the name of our Saviour who
was born in a stable. Amen.

PRAYER FROM HAWAII: *ANOTHER DAY*, CARDEN

～

Refugees

Mary and Joseph were forced to go to
  Egypt after Jesus was born;
It's as though you, O God, became a
  refugee.
Be the strength and comfort
to all refugees in our own age,
that they may eventually
find a home and find the peace
they long for.

∽

The Crucifixion

Lord Jesus, you suffered so much pain
and cruelty on the cross, but through it
all you held on to love. Be with us
whenever life is very, very tough and
keep us loving no matter what happens
— for that is your way — the way that
leads to peace and truth.

∽

The example of Jesus

Blessed Lord, you bore on the shameful
cross an undeserved punishment, and
forgave even those who nailed you
there. You spoke comfort to those who
were dying beside you, even during
your own agony. Teach us your love
and compassion. We can only hope to
follow your example if you guide us
every step of the way.

WORDS FOR WORSHIP, A. G. BULLIVANT

∽

Nothing conquers love
They spat at you, O Lord,
threw their venom in your face,
slapped and buffeted your body,
taunted and ridiculed your soul,
but through it all,
through the pain and the tears,
you held on to love,
and nothing they did could conquer
your eternal trust in God,
who brought you up from the darkness
  of death
to be the light and saviour of us all.

≈

Easter day
Lord Jesus, Lord of the Dance, you
have broken the gates of death and
released us from its terrors; spring up
within our lives that we may be your
Easter people and sing our 'Alleluias'
today, tomorrow and for ever.

≈

Mary Magdalen
Risen Lord Jesus, as Mary Magdalen
  met you in the garden
on the morning of your resurrection,
so may we meet you today and every
  day:
speak to us as you spoke to her;
reveal yourself as the living Lord;
renew our hope and kindle our joy;

≈

and send us to share the good news
  with others.

∾

Risen Jesus
Lord Jesus Christ,
risen from the tomb,
your love is let loose in the world;
let your love conquer my heart
that I may become one of your
  disciples
and follow you for ever . . .

∾

The light of Christ
The light of Christ pierces the darkness
  like a sword.
The light of Christ banishes the
  darkness like a fire.
The light of Christ conquers the
  darkness like a victorious army.
O light of Christ,
Shine in our hearts and lives
and bring us your life and your eternal
  victory.

∾

'Supposing him to be the gardener'
Often we don't recognize you, Lord,
even when you are very close: open our
eyes to see your love and power in the
world.

∾

Easter Day
Into that house they shall enter
and in that house they shall dwell
where there shall be
    no cloud or nor sun
    no darkness nor dazzling
but one equal light;
    no noise or silence
but one equal music;
    no fears or hopes
but one equal possession;
    no foes nor friends
but one equal eternity.

Keep us, Lord,
so awake in the duties of our callings
that we may thus sleep in thy peace
and wake in thy glory.

JOHN DONNE

～

More like Christ
O Christ risen and glorified,
reigning at God's right hand,
but still our Friend and Saviour,
abide with us,
so that by the loving influence
of your Spirit on our own,
we may become more like you;
until all our selfishness and unkindness
are purged away, and we become
the kind of people whom you can use

122

～

in your redeeming and glorious work.
Take possession of us now
and use us henceforth for your glory.
For your name's sake.

LESLIE WEATHERHEAD: *PRAYERS FOR PILGRIMS*, PAWLEY

~

Happiness at Easter

O Lord Jesus, I want to be happy
today, and to love you more than I
have ever done before, because you
must have been happy on that Easter
Day so many years ago, and must have
been so glad to know that your friends
would be happy once again. You
suffered and died because of your love
for us, and now that suffering is over
and you are with God in Heaven. Keep
us in your care, and make us more like
you, so that we may live with you for
ever.

~

Whitsun: the Holy Spirit

Lord, your life is let loose in our
world, making things new, bringing us
peace, giving us hope. We offer you our
'Hoorays' for your Holy Spirit.

~

'Like a dove'
A dove is white, pure . . .
Be gently around us like a cloud of
  white doves,
O Lord, our beautiful God.

≈

Tongues of fire
Fire is red and burning and very
  powerful . . .
O God, warm our hearts and our lives
that we may radiate your love
to the world, for Jesus' sake.

≈

Harvest: the fruits of the earth
Heavenly Creator and Lord of the world,
you have given us the soil, in all its richness,
to be the source of our food. Bless those
who care for the earth, that it may
always be fruitful and good for our use.

≈

The sounds of a bakery
For the soft murmur of flour:
We thank you, O God.
For the shake and rattle of salt:
We thank you, O God.
For the slap and bang of kneading
  dough:
We thank you, O God.
For the 'oohs' and 'aahs' as we eat
  warm bread:
We thank you, O God.

124

≈

Farmers
Bless with your wisdom and patience,
dear God, the farmers of the world,
that they may work with you and your
creation for the good of all.

~

Fish-harvest
Plaice, mackerel, haddock and cod,
These are the fish we eat, O God.
For prawns and shrimps, sardines on
    toast,
Praise Father, Son and Holy Ghost . . .

~

Garden chair
Lord, thank you for the pleasure
of sitting and looking,
and being quiet and still.
Teach us to appreciate the peace of your
    world,
and we may have peace in our hearts.

~

First the seed
Quietly the seed falls on the ground
  and dies
and waits for the warmth of spring;
then new life forces its way out of the
  darkness
and into the fresh bright air.
O God of death,
O God of life,
we praise you for the hope and harvest
  of the world.

~

Beautiful country
The green fields stretch up to the edge
  of the hills,
in the hedges birds sing,
and in the meadows sheep and cattle
  graze.
Ours is a beautiful country,
so forgive us, Lord, when we take it for
  granted
and show us how we may share our
  riches
with those who are poor,
and bring food to the starving,
and hope and peace to those who are in
  despair.

~

A blessing for travellers

May the road rise to meet you.
May the wind be always at your back.
May the sun shine warm upon your
    face,
the rains fall soft upon your fields and,
until we meet again,
may God hold you in the palm of his
    hand.

TRADITIONAL CELTIC BLESSING

~

To all who are travelling

To those who are travelling, good Lord,
give a fair journey, whether by air, or
land or sea, by river, lake or road.
Go with them on the way, to give
them back to their own people in
happiness and health.

DAWN THROUGH OUR DARKNESS, GILES HARCOURT

~

Trust in God

Lord, there's a journey ahead of me
but help me to know
that wherever I go
I can never be beyond your care.

~

Always there
In thy journeys to and fro
God direct thee;
In thy happiness and pleasure
God bless thee;
In care, anxiety, or trouble
God sustain thee;
In peril and danger
God protect thee.

ARCHBISHOP TIMOTHY OLWFOSOYE:
ANOTHER DAY, CARDEN

~

Giving gifts
With the tender and shy beauty of a
    gazelle
you came to us, O Lord,
quietly revealing the holy love of God.
As you have given yourself to us in
    gentleness,
may we give ourselves to others
and share with them your peace.

~

Receiving gifts
Help us, O Lord,
to receive all our gifts
with the generous and open-hearted joy
that comes from knowing
that all life is a gift of love
from you.

~

Teach us, good Lord

Teach us, good Lord, to serve thee as
    thou deservest:
to give and not to count the cost;
to fight and not to heed the wounds;
to toil and not to seek for rest;
to labour and not to ask for any
    rewards,
save that of knowing that we do thy
    will.

ST IGNATIUS LOYOLA

~

Christ in you

Christ has no body now on earth but
yours, no hands but yours, no feet but
yours; yours are the eyes through
which to look at Christ's compassion to
the world, yours are the feet with
which he is to go about doing good,
and yours are the hands with which he
is to bless us now.

ST TERESA

~

God our Friend and Helper

God our Friend and Helper

Although the world is very beautiful, sometimes it is also a place of suffering. There are natural disasters, like earthquakes, hurricanes and volcanoes. And there are man-made disasters like wars and famines.

How can we go on believing in a God of love when we see so much suffering?

Christians believe that in Jesus, God takes pain and suffering on himself and shares them with us. In doing so he shows us the real way to live – giving ourselves completely to the importance of love.

Prayer is a way of bearing suffering, knowing that God is in the heart of it with us, wanting to bring us his healing and love.

You have examined me and you know
    me.
You know everything I do;
from faraway you understand all my
    thoughts.
You see me, whether I am working or
    resting;
you know all my actions.

Even before I speak,
you already know what I will say.
You are around me on every side;
you protect me with your power.
Your knowledge of me is too deep;
it is beyond my understanding.

Where could I go to escape from you?
Where could I get away from your
    presence?
If I went up to heaven, you would be
    there;
if I lay down in the world of the dead,
you would be there.
If I flew away beyond the east
or lived in the farthest place in the
    west,
you would be there to lead me,
you would be there to help me.
I could ask the darkness to hide me
or the light round me to turn into
    night,
but even darkness is not dark for you,
and the night is as bright as the day.
Darkness and light are the same to you.

You created every part of me;
you put me together in my mother's
    womb.
I praise you because you are to be
    feared;
all you do is strange and wonderful.

I know it with all my heart.
When my bones were being formed,
carefully put together in my mother's
    womb,
when I was growing there in secret,
you knew that I was there —
you saw me before I was born.
The days allotted to me
had all been recorded in your book,
before any of them ever began.

PSALM 139:1–16

~

God helps in times of trouble
God, you are our father, always with
us, giving us strength, bringing us
hope. Thank you for your love which
never fails us nor forsakess us; for you
are a faithful and most loving friend.

~

When I am unhappy
When I am unhappy, Lord,
help me to share my troubles with you.
You'll understand why I am crying,
and that will be comforting to know.

HELLO GOD, WINN

~

Disasters
We saw the pictures on the television of
. . . . Lord God, be the strength of all
those who are in terrible sorrow, that
they may be helped in their despair and
find your light, even where all seems to
be utter darkness.

~

Tears
Almighty God, Father of all mankind,
in your Son you took upon yourself the
world's sorrow.
We offer you our own sorrow and
sadness, knowing that you can help us
to bear our grief through the infinite
understanding and love of Jesus Christ
our Lord.

~

By and by all things
By and by all things must die,
We know this is so.
Animals, birds, the flowers, the trees,
People we love, those whose lives we
   share —
This is the hardest loss to bear.
When we are sad, Lord, you are there,
Loving and understanding.

HELLO GOD, WINN

136
~

For the river

Protect, O Lord, all those who fish in
the rivers and creeks of this country.
Give strength to their arms as they
paddle their canoes and cast their nets.
Grant them success in their work. In
the anxious hours of waiting, steady
and support them, and grant that in
dangers often, in watching often, in
weariness often, they may have a quiet
mind; through Jesus Christ our Lord.

MORNING, NOON & NIGHT

Work in the harbour

The day is there and the sunshine,
With the steamers in the harbour,
But is there work?
Others have friends,
Others have money.
And I stand nearby unemployed.
Dear God, can't you give me work in
    the harbour?
To have money for wife and children.
To put my little bit in your basket next
    Sunday.
Please give me work, good Lord Jesus.
We praise you. Amen

OXFORD BOOK OF PRAYER

The blind
Almighty God, Father of all mankind,
embrace the blind with your love, that
they may feel your presence in their
inmost souls and know your guiding
hand, through Jesus Christ, our Lord.

~

Hands who touched the leper
Hands who touched the leper,
touch my wounded heart;
Hands who healed the blind man,
heal my aching soul;
Hands who cured the lame,
mend my disjointed life;
Hands who embraced all life,
enfold me in your peace.
Lord,
merely touch and heal,
cure and forgive.

SHORT PRAYERS FOR THE LONG DAY,
GILES AND MELVILLE HARCOURT

~

Mentally handicapped people
Help us, O God, to enter gently into
the world of mentally handicapped
people, that in humility we may learn
from them, and share with them, in the
beauty and mystery of your world.

~

Prayer of a disabled child
Lord, you were disabled
when you hung on the cross;
yet that is how you showed us
God's love.
May the power of that love
shine through my weakness,
my disability, to show
God's glory to the world.

PUFFIN BOOK OF PRAYERS

~

Prisoners
We pray, O Father, for those whose
freedom has been taken from them; for
all who suffer imprisonment, whether
for crime or for conscience's sake; for
all whose vision of your world is seen
through bars, and in whose heart the
lamp of hope burns low. God of mercy,
give them help, according to their need,
and hear our prayer for Jesus Christ's
sake.

DAILY PRAYER

~

Working for peace
Today, O God, I'm going to do
    something for peace.
If someone shouts, I shan't answer
    back;
If someone is rude, I shan't be rude to
    them;
If someone says something spiteful, I
    shall ignore them.
I know it's not much, O God,
but with your blessing maybe it will
    help.

Different races
Here we are, O God,
all the peoples of the world,
all the colours of the rainbow . . .
Be present among us so that we may
enjoy our differences,
and work together for the good of all.

Prayer for peace
Lord Jesus, we pray for peace at all
times. Whenever there is a war, we pray
that people will have peace in their
hearts. Amen.

War
The tank lumbered into the town
crushing cars, splintering fences,
it was so ugly, so unstoppable;
Lord, forgive our cruelty.
The sniper aimed his rifle
with intense and evil precision
and in the street a woman fell.

Lord, forgive our evil.

The terrorist placed a bomb
in a holdall in the shopping precinct
and walked away casually.

Lord, forgive our wickedness.

Wherever there is cruelty,
change our hearts to hearts of peace
Wherever there is evil,
change our hearts to hearts of goodness
Wherever there is wickedness,
bring repentance and pardon, for Jesus'
    sake.

∽

Live in peace
Dear Father in heaven, let the power of
    your peace
rest upon those who make war,
that they may learn to live in peace
and be at peace with everyone.

∽

Fill our hearts with love
Lord God, take from our hearts all
anger, pain and bitterness, and teach us
how to forgive, so that we may share in
your healing love for the world.

~

Saying something helpful
God grant that when the chance to say
something helpful comes our way, we
shall be brave enough to say it.

WORDS FOR WORSHIP

~

Unkind words
Gracious Lord, help us to refrain from
speaking unkind words, so that we may
be known for our words of kindness.

WORDS FOR WORSHIP

~

Words
Word of God, give me the words to
 praise you for ever and ever.

~

Communication
Father, you spoke the word and the
universe came to life. Teach us to use
words with respect and care, knowing
the great good and the great harm that
words can do.

~

God our Father
God our Father of the world,
please help us to love one another.
Make nations friendly with other
   nations.
Make all of us love one another.
Help us to do our part to bring peace
   in the world
and happiness to all men.

HELLO GOD, WINN

~

A new world
God, what kind of world is this
that the adult people
are going to leave for us children?
There is fighting everywhere
and they tell us we live in a time of
   peace.
You are the only one who can help us.
Lord, give us a new world
in which we can be happy,
in which we can have friends
and work together for a good future.
A world in which there will not be
any cruel people
who seek to destroy us and our world
in so many ways.
Amen.

WRITTEN BY A LIBERIAN CHILD: *ANOTHER DAY*, CARDEN

~

Home
Father of all mankind, make the roof of
my house wide enough for all opinions,
oil the door of my house so it opens
easily to friend and stranger, and set
such a table in my house that my
whole family may speak kindly and
freely around it. Amen.

PRAYER FROM HAWAII: *ANOTHER DAY*, CARDEN

Endings

Endings

When the day has finally drawn to its close, it is time to look back over all that has happened and to thank God for his presence. Then we can rest sweetly in the calm of his love.

Prayer is a way of reflecting on times that have passed, and of looking forward to the future.

Safe
Dear Jesus, as a hen covers her chicks
with her wings to keep them safe, do
thou this dark night protect us under
your golden wings.

PRAYER FROM INDIA: *ANOTHER DAY*, CARDEN

Thy child
Come, O Father, here I am: let us go
   on.
I know that my words are those of a
   child;
but it is *Thy* child that prays to Thee.
It is *Thy* dark I walk in, it is *Thy* hand
   I hold.

GEORGE MACDONALD: *ANOTHER DAY*, CARDEN

Peace
Save us, O Lord, waking; guard us
    sleeping;
That awake we may watch with Christ,
And asleep we may rest in peace.

TRADITIONAL

~

Time for bed
Good night, dear Lord, and may I say,
Thank you for another day.
Keep me safe tonight, I pray,
And eager for tomorrow.
May I grow up kind and caring,
Joyfully your blessings sharing,
Following the way you tread.
Thank you, Lord, it's time for bed.
Amen.

HELLO GOD, WINN

~

Security
Lord, keep us safe this night,
Secure from all our fears.
May angels guard us while we sleep
Till morning light appears.

~

Light in the dark
Be a light in the dark for us,
dear Lord, we pray,
and as we lie sleeping
keep evil away.

PRAYERS FOR CHILDREN, J. LAIRD

148

~

Gone is the sun
The day is done,
Gone is the sun,
Dear Father, bless us every one.

HELLO GOD, WINN

~

Sleep in peace
O Heavenly Father, protect and bless all
things that have breath. Guard them
from evil and let them sleep in peace.

ALBERT SCHWEITZER

~

Blessings

Blessings

A blessing is a way of putting into words the good intention and love of God. It's like sunshine streaming out over the world.

Prayer is a way of working with God so that the whole earth may be blessed by God's love and peace.

Pilgrim's prayer
O God our Father
And his son Jesu Christ
And the Holy Spirit,
May you give me blessing while in this world,
while you lead me through the forests,
through the lakes and the mountains,
so that I may do your work among your people.
Grant that I may be loved by you;
and your people.

PRAYERS FOR PILGRIMS, PAWLEY

Held by God
Lord, you hold our world in your
  hands,
you hold my family in your hands,
you hold me in your hands,
and bring to us all the blessing of your
  love.

~

At rest
Let hope be my shield,
let love be my helmet,
let peace be my breastplate,
and then, blessed by hope, blessed by
  love,
blessed by peace,
I can be at rest.

~

My helper
O God, be my guardian
Stay always with me
In the morning
In the evening
By day or by night
Be my helper.

HELLO GOD, WINN

~

Like dew on grass
God, let your blessing rest upon us
like the dew on the grass,
bringing refreshment, beauty and joy
to body, mind and soul.

154

~

The Lord bless us

The Lord bless us and keep us;
the Lord make his face shine upon us
and be gracious unto us:
the Lord lift up his countenance upon us,
and give us peace.

TRADITIONAL

~

The blessing of God

God the Father, bless us;
God the Son, defend us;
God the Spirit, keep us
Now and evermore.

TRADITIONAL

~

The strength of God

May the strength of God pilot us,
May the power of God preserve us,
May the wisdom of God instruct us,
May the hand of God protect us,
May the way of God direct us,
May the shield of God defend us,
May the hosts of God guard us against
    the snares
of evil and the temptations of the world.

ST PATRICK

~

A guide

Be Thou a bright flame before me,
Be Thou a guiding star above me,
Be Thou a smooth path below me,
And a kindly shepherd behind me,
Today, tonight and forever.

ST COLUMBA

~

God be in my head

God be in my head,
And in my understanding;
God be in mine eyes,
And in my looking;
God be in my mouth,
And in my speaking;
God be in my heart,
And in my thinking;
God be at mine end,
And at my departing.

BOOK OF HOURS

~

Paradise

Jesus Christ, thou child so wise,
Bless mine hands and fill mine eyes
And bring my soul to paradise.

HILAIRE BELLOC

~

Index

158

161

Acknowledgements

The author and publisher would like to thank the following for their kind permission to reprint copyright material in this book.

Prayers from another day: Carden, SPCK
Prayers for Pilgrims: Pawley, SPCK
Morning, Noon & Night: Church Missionary Society
A Private House of Prayer: Leslie Weatherhead, Edward England Literary Agency
Oxford Book of Prayer: Appleton, OUP
Prayers for every day: Vicars Bell, OUP
Daily Prayer: Briggs & Milner-White, OUP
Mrs M. Davis: Marlborough
Hello Jesus: Sayer, Kevin Mayhew Ltd, Licence No. 397060
Words for Worship: Campling & Davis, Edward Arnold (Hodder & Stoughton)
Hello God: Alison Winn, Word Publishing (UK)
Good News Bible: Bible Society
'Scriptures quoted from the International Children's Bible, New Century Edition (Anglicised edition) copyright © 1991 by Word (UK) Ltd, Milton Keynes, England. Used by permission'.